ENDORSEMENTS

Tanner Olson's *Continue* is a gift. It is written for such a time as this. It is important. It is on time. It is just what I needed, and I am guessing it is just what you need too. There is art you can look at. This is art you can read. But it is more than art. It is a guide to being with God, talking with Him, and letting Him give you the gifts He is already offering. Tanner's writings and poems reminded me of what is always true but what I often forget. Take a deep breath, let it out, and enjoy having hope again.

—REV. GREG FINKE
Author of *Joining Jesus on His Mission*

Tanner is a poet in the most biblical sense of the word. He writes in such a way that his words can enter depths of joy or sadness and provide hope anchored in Christ. His poems can also be a blessing on a Tuesday when the dishes are still dirty, you forgot to bring in the garbage can from the curb, and you're just ready to go to bed. In both those things, there is deep beauty. *Continue* offers prayers as poetry, and it will be a blessing for you as you trust and follow Jesus.

—REV. TED DOERING
Pastor of Narrative Lutheran Church, Round Rock, TX;
co-author of *Myth of the Millennial*; author of *Walking Together:*
Simple Steps for Discipleship

Continue reminds us of an important yet easily forgotten truth: faith in Jesus isn't just for good days and bad days—it is woven into every day. Tanner's poetry elevates the ordinary and allows us to see it with fresh eyes, recognizing the goodness of God carrying us through the simple, small, and normal stuff of life.

—REV. MATT POPOVITS
Lead pastor of St. Mark Houston, Houston, TX

Tanner gives unique, beautiful, and honest words navigating what faith looks like in a constantly changing world. This collection of poems will help you see that despite change all around us, God is here, God is in control, and God is deeply in love with you. You may laugh at some poems, you may cry at others, and still others will likely leave you in deep thought. Tanner is a masterful wordsmith, and I highly recommend this resource for anyone seeking to grow in their faith.

—REV. ZACH ZEHNDER
Teaching pastor at King of Kings in Omaha, NE;
founder of Red Letter Living and
author of the best-selling *Red Letter Challenge*

Tanner Olson, as always, continues to bring words of hope both in our happiness and our heartbreak. Tanner's gift is being able to honor both, speaking God's truth and grace in each moment.

—DCS. HEIDI GOEHMANN
Licensed clinical social worker and mental health care provider;
theologian, writer, and advocate;
author of *Emotions & the Gospel: Created for Connection*

Tanner is one of the most prolific and reflective Christian poets of this day and age. His ability to take thought that is abstract, floating in the minds of all of us, and to put words to that which is intangible—it is akin to praying as a community together. Expressing many emotions at once to God and knowing that in each verse God hears us—catching each verse with His almighty hands. Tanner's work is a gift to God's people, the Church, and our broken world.

—REV. DR. GERARD BOLLING
Assistant professor of leadership and
theology at Concordia University Texas;
associate pastor at Bethlehem Lutheran Church, St. Louis, MO

ACKNOWLEDGMENTS

To Sarah. You make everything better. Thanks for saying yes to this life together.

To my family, friends, and teachers. I wouldn't be here if it wasn't for your love, kindness, and patience. I started listing each of you by name, but it turned into a second book. You know who you are. And if you don't think it's you, it is.

To Jamie, Anna, Elizabeth, Laura, Alex, and the entire staff at CPH for your dedication to this project.

To my Patreon and online community. Thank you for believing in my work and for supporting this calling. May we continue to remember that hope doesn't let our story end.

Thanks be to God for the beautiful gifts of this world: hope, dogs, pop-punk music, grace, basketball, coffee, cinnamon rolls, sunshine. Without these gifts this book would never have happened.

To Christ alone.

Published by Concordia Publishing House

3558 S. Jefferson Avenue, St. Louis, MO 63118-3968

1-800-325-3040 ● cph.org

Library of Congress Cataloging-in-Publication Data
Names: Olson, Tanner, 1989 author.
Title: Continue : poems and prayers of hope / Tanner Olson.
Description: St. Louis, MO : Concordia Publishing House, [2022] | Summary: "Poems and prayers to inspire hope in the day-to-day of ordinary life. These accessible, faith-based poems encourage readers to trust God and to take the next step with faith despite questions, difficulties, and fears"—Provided by publisher.
Identifiers: LCCN 2022002788 (print) | LCCN 2022002789 (ebook) | ISBN 9780758672230 (paperback) | ISBN 9780758672247 (ebook)
Subjects: LCGFT: Religious poetry.
Classification: LCC PS3615.L75276 C66 2022 (print) | LCC PS3615.L75276 (ebook) | DDC 811/.6--dc23/eng/20220225
LC record available at https://lccn.loc.gov/2022002788
LC ebook record available at https://lccn.loc.gov/2022002789

1 2 3 4 5 6 7 8 9 10   31 30 29 28 27 26 25 24 23 22

• • •

CONTINUE

POEMS & PRAYERS OF HOPE
TANNER OLSON

CONCORDIA PUBLISHING HOUSE • SAINT LOUIS

INTRODUCTION

A Few Thoughts on Prayer (and Poetry)

God,
won't You again draw near?
Because again I need to hear
despite the pain and fear
You are here.

Most of my prayers begin with an audible exhale.
I pull the air through my nose into the depths
of my body and let it rest there.
For a moment, I'm full
before I slowly breathe out.
The heaviness of another day exits my body, leaving me
empty but ready.
And then I begin to pray.

Praying looks different for me these days.
I'm asking God more questions and sitting longer with the
silence.
I trust He doesn't need my words, but still wants to hear
from me, like a father or mother wants to hear from their
child.

Distractions bid for my attention;
I fight not to stare at my phone or get caught up in the
clouds passing by.

I'm restless.
I've always been restless.
But restlessness has turned into wrestling.
Wrestling with what is and what will be and how and
when and where and so on.
Maybe you're wrestling too.
So I'll continue to pray.
And listen.
And plea.
And ask.
And wonder.
And wrestle.
And trail off.
And start again.
And again.
And again.
I will pray, just like Jesus did in the Garden.
I will continue to believe He is doing something more
than I can see.
Because He is.
He is doing more than I can see.
He is doing more than we can see.
He is.

And He is, as I am coming to see, always ready to listen
or welcome me into the comfort of His silence.

The invitation to speak with God
is like Waffle House:
always open, no matter what.
An open hand outstretched to sit and be with the Giver of
grace.

I used to think God only heard our prayers if
our hands were folded, head bowed, and eyes closed.
Sometimes I fold my hands while I pray.
Sometimes I bow my head.
But I have a hard time keeping my eyes closed.
Praying is less like math and science and more
like art, like poetry.
God isn't grading us or checking our work.
He isn't looking for mistakes or skipped steps.
He's listening.
He's taking in what we say.
He's admiring.

Tomorrow as the sun creeps over the
trees, I'll slowly inhale and exhale.
I'll sit in silence before I speak.
In the quiet of the morning,
I'll bring God my honest thoughts and thanks.

I'll ask for forgiveness and help, just like
the day before, just like tomorrow.

And as I go, I'll hold hope close,
knowing He hears me,
knowing He loves me,
knowing He's with me.

Moment by moment.
Day by day.
Season by season.
He hears me.
He loves me.
He is with me.

How to Use This Book

This book is not a map or textbook. It doesn't read like a novel or ancient text. What you are holding is a collection of prayers, poems, and writings.

And it's yours.

There are no rules for this book.

You can read it in one sitting or over the next ten years. You can keep this book at your bedside or in the bathroom. You can earmark pages, underline words, and make notes.

Perhaps there will be a page written for you or a loved one. Don't hesitate to send the words found in this book to a friend in need of prayer and hope.

As you read, take a moment to reflect and contemplate on the words. Let these pages meet you where you are and as you are. Some of the poems and prayers will sound different from your traditional way of praying, but let them not escape you.

When you read, I encourage you to ask the Spirit to move and guide You.

I pray the words on these pages will draw you closer to God, lead you back to Scripture, and point you to the ultimate source of hope, Jesus Christ.

God Is Here

There is something about pausing and saying,
"God is here."

I've been starting my mornings by whispering
these three words to myself.

A beautiful reminder that you are not alone.
The Creator of the world sees you and knows you and is
with you.

God is here.

Some days I wake with a mind that doesn't
seem to grasp the meaning of rest.
Or stillness.
Or peace.

And so I pray.
Or I try to pray.

I take a few deep breaths.

I let the silence meet me where I am.

I picture the light breaking through the darkness.

I don't know why, but that's what I picture.

It's holy and peaceful and promising.

I guess that's why.

I invite my head to unfold like my
hands and hand it all over.
To no longer carry what my mind has gripped with
anxiousness and over-thinking and all the other things
that pull me from where I need to be.

My morning prayers are groggy thoughts seeking
a foundation, a place to stand tall in the confidence of a
forever hope.

In prayer I run to His outstretched arms,
reaching for His peace that passes all of my
understanding,
yet perfectly meets me where I am.

Peace perfectly meets me where I am.

My prayers aren't poetic or perfect,
but they don't need to be.

And when I say *amen*, I know then,
and only then, can I begin.

Today begins with *amen*.

I have set the LORD always before me; because He is at my
right hand, I shall not be shaken.

PSALM 16:8

Prayer

You don't have to paint a masterpiece;
you can color outside the lines.
There is nothing you need to bring to the table
but yourself.
Just bring yourself.
Your heart and silence and mess.
Not a time to compare or compete,
this is an open invitation to be
with the One who created you to be.
Here, you can listen and rest and thank and speak.
He has invited you.

Morning Prayer

Lord,

You are the center of my everything.
Let my eyes ever be on You.
Let my heart be changed by You.
Let my hands be moved by You.
Let my soul be stirred by You.
Give me strength to surrender and eyes to see this life
is not about me.
May all of this always be for You.

Amen.

In All Things

Between it all and through it all,
You have always been in it all.
For You are in all things.
The beginning and becoming.
The pain and problems.
The anxiety and assurance.
The wrestle and rest.
The beauty and mess.
You are in the sunrises and sunsets and storms between.
The steps forward and steps back.
You are in my hope and joy, suffering and sadness.
The known and unknown, certain and uncertain.
You are in it all because of Your great love for all.

You came to restore and reunite all things to Yourself.
To satisfy our souls; to be our glory; to be the hope for the
world.

No shame or sin or doubt can keep us from You.
Through the blood of the cross and the empty tomb,
You have made peace and promise us a forever in Your
hands.

The same hands that placed the sun, moon, and
stars in the sky placed the spark in our eyes.
The hands that hold yesterday, today, and tomorrow also
hold our dreams and sorrow.

The hands that were nailed to the tree have thrown away
our sins and set us free.
And the hands that hold all things hold me as I am.

There is nothing outside of You.

All things are for You and from You and through You
and that includes me.
I am not forgotten.
Now and forever, I am in Your hands.

And again I'll remember,
between it all and through it all,
You have always been in it all.

Goodness

You've set goodness ahead of me.
Tomorrow when I wake it will be waiting for me.
And the next day.
And the next.
When I turn around I'll see You've placed goodness
behind me too.
It may not look the way I think it will, but it's there.
I am followed by Your love and mercy.
Every step.
Every breath.
Every moment.
Your goodness is constant and I am constantly
surrounded by Your goodness.

Pick Up Love

May these hands
release control
and pick up love.

The Softness of Grace

Let the softness of grace
bring you forward and through
and guide you from place to place.

Let it remind you
softness is strength
rooted in hope.

May this grace
bring you to rest
and breathe
and remember:
He has set you free.

May It Be So

Steal away the fear.
Silence the doubt.
Comfort the pain.
Meet the madness.
As only You do, God.
May it be so.

New

I walked up the street toward the rising sun.
Again I couldn't sleep.
My mind was moving and I decided my feet should as
well.
Light slowly pushed the dark aside as I climbed the hill
outside our home.
Shadows followed as the late fall breeze rolled toward me.
I pushed my hands deep into my pockets and pressed on.
I inhaled, closing my eyes for one step, two.
Cool air scratched down my lungs.
I watched my breath escape before now-open eyes.
I thanked God,
the start of my morning prayer.

I felt known.

I felt new.

An invitation to begin again.

And Forever

God, be my strength.
God, be my hope.
God, be my joy.
Today, tomorrow, and forever.

I Don't Doubt You

It isn't that I doubt You or Your faithfulness.
I am wondering what will become.
What I thought would be by now feels far from ever
happening.
And I am having trouble letting go and moving on because
the last thing I want to do is let go and move on.
But it's time.
Time to mourn the loss of what will never be found,
to bring forward what is inside and lay it down,
to ask You again to lead me to solid ground.
Guide me out of the shadows and into Your light.
Open my eyes to see and believe You've always had
something different for me.
And different isn't bad, but beautiful.
It's beautiful.

When There Are No Words

God,
I don't know.
Amen.

It Is the Light

When it feels like the end
keep looking
for where the light comes in,
because it is the light
that reminds us
we can continue
again.

Again Jesus spoke to them, saying, "I am the light of the world. Whoever follows Me will not walk in darkness, but will have the light of life."

J O H N   8 : 1 2

Slowly Grew

When I look back I can see
how season after season
slowly grew me to be
the person I have become.

With patience and grace,
You slowly grew me to be,
moving my eyes to the light,
a reminder there is more to this life.

And when I look ahead
I am beginning to see
I am far from done.

Whatever You Have for Me: A Prayer for Now

Lord,

Whatever You have for me today, may
I accept it with open hands.
Give me the courage to love and forgive,
to be a person of peace.
Take my eyes off where I am not and place them on where
You have me.
Help me trust that whatever You have for me is for my
good.
When I worry, may I remember You know me.
You know my needs and dreams and fears and everything
in-between and beyond.
Through it all, Jesus, You are with me.
Right now, You are with me.

Amen.

And This Is Not Easy

I am coming to see
life isn't what I thought
it was going to be.

And this is not easy.

To let go of dreams you came to know,
to watch the world change and yours stay the same,
to grieve what you never received.

It is not easy.

But I am not done.

I am slowly accepting that despite
what has come or failed to be,
You still love me.
You still see me.
You still hear me.
You still care for me.

God, I pray this will be enough for me.

Why

Why do I worry?
Christ is with me.

Why do I fight?
Christ is within me.

Why do I fear?
Christ is behind me.

Why do I doubt?
Christ is before me.

Spirit

Spirit,

With Your hand of comfort, draw me
deeper into Your presence.
Open my hands to hold and give hope.
Tune my ears and ready my feet to go where You lead.
Protect me from all harm and temptation.
Place Your song of joy in my soul as I go through light and
darkness, day and night.
Let Your grace move me,
Your love humble me,
Your will be done.

Amen.

Heaven

On days that feel like the end, the hope of heaven remains
constant as I continue to find my way in this world.

Place me in the shadow of Your conquered cross
and fill me with the hope of Your empty tomb.

Spirit, breathe wonder and life into my weary bones
as I trust and step and shake into the unknown.

God, lead me in the light of Your forgiveness as
the echoes of glorious grace guide me home.

As Your mercy follows me, touch my brokenness with joy.

Lift my eyes above; let my lips sing holy.

May they never cease to sing holy, holy, holy.

For You are.

From beginning to end, You are holy, holy, holy.

God Is

In my frustration, God remains patient.
In my discomfort, God remains kind.
In my waiting, God remains present.
In my wondering, God remains good.
In my anger, God remains loving.
In my doubt, God remains faithful.

Joy Continues

Joy of my salvation continues to light the darkest of
places, breaks through the heaviness to remind me new
beginnings are found even on Tuesdays.
There has always been joy.
Before and during and after the storm.
In heartbreak.
Or sickness.
Or change.
Or uncertainty.
There always seems to be something.
And something else.
Just like there always seems to be joy.
There has always been joy.

Even in this.

Count it all joy, my brothers, when you meet trials of various kinds, for you know that the testing of your faith produces steadfastness. And let steadfastness have its full effect, that you may be perfect and complete, lacking in nothing.

JAMES 1:2–4

Faithful

Move me to be
faithful in the waiting,
faithful in the wondering,
faithful in the wandering.

How Long, O Lord?

When I read *How long, O Lord*,
the words wrap around my soul,
like they were written for me or by me,
a hug from an old friend.
They saw me where I was, knowing where I wanted to be
but wasn't.

At least not yet.

Maybe ever.

I don't know how to get where I want to be.
You cannot force life to happen.
At least, I'm learning you can't.

I wait and hope and pray for an answer or for change.
I've lost count of how long it has been, but it feels too
long.
The world blooms around me while I'm left in winter.
To my left and right I see beauty unfold, wondering when
it will fall on me.

The world is too big to feel trapped, but I do.
But while I wait I look back and see how wonderfully
He has led me and loved me.

He has not brought me this far to leave
me alone in my war within.

Every morning, even today, the worst of days,
I raise my eyes and thank Him with trust.
For He, even in this, somehow in this, is still good.
In the sorrow, rejoicing looks like exhaling
and taking one more step.
Like trusting something more is happening.

And so again I pray,
How long, O Lord?
How long?

How long, O Lord? Will You forget me forever? How long
will You hide Your face from me?

PSALM 13:1

Wherever I Am, You Are Too

Where I am is the
last place I thought I'd be,
but maybe this is
where I need to be,
because wherever I am
You are too.

Fear not, for I am with you; be not dismayed, for I am your
God; I will strengthen you, I will help you, I will uphold you
with My righteous right hand.

ISAIAH 41:10

Another Step Forward

Father,

May it be with grace.
May it be with peace.
May it be with hope.
May it be with love.
May it be with mercy.
May You be our strength
as we take another step forward.

Amen.

For When You Forget

He is still Lord over all.
He is still listening when we pray.
He is still holding all things together.
His mercies are still new every morning.
He is still for us.
He is still forgiving.
He still says, "Come to Me."
His tomb is still open and empty.
The Light is still breaking through the darkness.
He is still calling us beloved.
He is still giving us rest.
He is still inviting us to cast our anxieties on Him,
to love our neighbors as ourselves.
He is still our strength when we are weak.
He is still removing our sins as far as the east is from the
west.
He is still good.
He is still sending us.
He is still with us.
He is still the beginning and the end.
He is still coming again.

With Peace

Inhale: Trust
Exhale: Peace

In Christ alone, I trust I can live today with peace
without knowing what tomorrow brings.

I Believe He Hears What I Don't Say Out Loud

From the outside, you couldn't hear what I was saying, but
I was saying something.
And I believe He heard me.
Thoughts of thanksgiving
and wonderings of living
and the silence between the two,
He hears it all.
I don't know how.
Perhaps it's like sonar or our thoughts dance and play on a
frequency only God hears.
Somehow, some way, I believe He hears me,
the trapped whispers and shattering shouts
rising and falling in the silence of my mind.
Maybe God puts His ear to the beat of my heart and
understands the movement of my soul.
Or maybe He is just God and knows to listen to the cries
of His child.

Either way, He hears me.

I don't know how.

But I do know a silent prayer can be quite loud.

———————————

Before they call I will answer; while they are yet speaking I will hear.

ISAIAH 65:24

A Little Closer

Lean in
a little closer
to hear
His love
spoken straight into
the fear.

———————————

There is no fear in love, but perfect love casts out fear. For fear has to do with punishment, and whoever fears has not been perfected in love.

1 JOHN 4:18

Even Through This

God,

Will You meet me in my wanting?

Will You lead me to rest in peace with You?

Will You walk with me through this darkness?

Again and again I'll say,
You are with me.

You are with me.
Where You are there is no fear.
Where You are there is comfort.
And I can see goodness is following me.
Even through this.
Even through this You are with me.

Amen.

Come and See

Come and see.
You are forgiven.
You are free.

He has taken
what you thought He wouldn't touch.

He has forgotten
what you cannot help but remember.

He has already done
what needed to be done.

And it was done
out of love.

Come and see.
You are forgiven.
You are free.

Free to live in peace.
Free to walk in love.
Free to go and tell of what He has done.

And Today

And today,
just like yesterday,
I will stand with faith
and press on anyway.

When the world echoes,
"This is the end,"
I'll breathe in deep,
remember Your holy name,
say *amen*,
and continue with faith once again.

You Remain

In seasons when I feel far from my faith,
I'll look up and count the ways
You've remained.
You've remained faithful.
And loving.
And kind.
You've remained merciful.
And inviting.
And present.

Through it all,
my doubts and fears,
silence and screams,
You've remained.

You Are

Give me the vision to see
and the courage to believe
that through every little thing
You are right beside me.

_____

And behold, I am with you always, to the end of the age.

MATTHEW 28:20

Before I Begin

Before I begin, I gather the quiet
and give to the world around me
an honest exhale.

I open my eyes to the light
and hand over what's in my hands
and ask God for His will to be done.

Some days I'm not sure what that means,
His will to be done,
but I know I mean it.

Out loud I say with confidence
that all I have and all I will become
is for Him and Him alone.

If all things are in His hands, then that is where I am too.

Safe and sound, seen and found.

Your will be done.

Forget

There is something about waking up before the world to
watch the sun rise.
To see the light slowly shake the earth awake, like my
mom would wake me before taking me
to second grade, gently rubbing my back,
telling her son to rise and shine.

These days, I've been trying to rise and
shine, but my glow isn't as bright;
something just doesn't feel quite right.

I don't know if it's the winter or my diet
or because I'm no longer in second grade.

Maybe it's seasonal depression or because I
spend too much time looking at my phone,
trying to find ways to feel less alone.

Or maybe, as long as I'm telling you everything, it's
because I don't feel like I'm doing enough or am enough.

I've got a long list of mistakes I play in my mind from
yesterday and the days before, but I'm also worried
about what's ahead and if the prayers I'm praying
will ever be heard or answered or just forgotten.

I'm scared of being forgotten.
But this morning, as I watched the light make its way
into our home, I began to remember that I am not
forgotten or alone.

The light found me.
I'm holding onto this.

I'm trying to remember to forget about
yesterday and to just be right where I am.
I'm trying to remember to forget about tomorrow and to
just be right where I am.
I'm just trying to be right where I am.
The light found me.

I'm holding onto this.

Hold onto this.

For the Sick

Lord,

Draw near and give rest.
Lay Your hand of comfort on all aches and pains and fears.
Fill wondering minds with the peace of Your promise.
Tune hearts to sing of Your mercy through the darkness
of night.
May joy be found in the morning, a reminder that renewal
comes in many ways, but it always comes from You.

Amen.

Continue

When I wake tomorrow
I'll do what I did today
with a little more experience.
A little more courage.
A little more faith.
A little more love.
I'll continue.
Every breath with grace
and every step for peace.
I'll continue.

Courage

Give me the courage

to believe everything I do has purpose.
to live out the truth with love.

to believe everything I say matters.
to live out love with joy.

Give me the courage
to step into another day with hope.

Again and Again

I've begun to let go of what was,
to lay the past down and turn around
to remind myself I was lost
but I've been found.

I'm starting to see it is better for me
to live in grace and walk in love
and fix my eyes on what is above.

Day after day
I continue to realize my hope is my home,
and we were never created to do this life alone.

Every day I wake
I thank Him that I can begin
again and again.

And you can begin
again and again.

_____

If then you have been raised with Christ, seek the things that are above, where Christ is, seated at the right hand of God. Set your minds on things that are above, not on things that are on earth. For you have died, and your life is hidden with Christ in God. When Christ who is your life appears, then you also will appear with Him in glory.

COLOSSIANS 3:1–4

The Character of God

Your love is louder than my fear.
Your mercy is greater than my past.
Your grace is, as it has always been,
enough.

For All

For all I have done.
For all I have felt.
For all I have feared.

There is grace.
There is hope.
There is love.
There is more to the story.

You Always Have

Sometimes I forget You know me better than I will ever know myself.

I forget Your compassion and loyalty and how when Jesus told the parable of the lost son, He wasn't just telling a story but was talking about us.

Telling us we are remembered and seen and loved.

We are.

Even when we think we aren't.

When I lose my way, which happens most every day, I am quick to ask why and slow to remember why.

It's because You love us.

God, You always have.

It's because You see something more in us than we see in ourselves.

You always have.

You've broken down my walls and ways and welcomed me home.

Now let me embrace the goodness of Your mercy and grace.

See What Happens

Once again I'll
slow down
and breathe deep
and look up
and say *amen*
and see what happens.

Fall Forward

Lord,

With every breath
and every step,
may I trust You
as I fall forward.

Amen.

Trust and Surrender

Won't You gently hear me once again as I pray these
words of trust and surrender?

Please use me.
Please send me.
Please move me.
Please hold me.
Please use my life.

Let all of this be for Your glory, Your good.

Give joy to these feet as they step into the unknown.

Give trust to these hands as they serve with love.

Give grace to my words as they echo
the good news of hope.

Like the Sheep

Gather my worries like the sheep.
Call them out of the wilderness and to Your side.
Lead them to a place where they can become free of my
hands.
They've been with me now for quite some time and I am
ready to leave them behind.
Hold them tight as I wave goodbye.
Keep them close as I step forward with peace.
As I leave them in Your care, replace them with
the joy You've always had for me.

Have Mercy on Me

As my eyes open to a new day,
have mercy on me.

As the sun meets the sky,
have mercy on me.

As the world wakes,
have mercy on me.

As the flowers bloom,
have mercy on me.

As the work piles up,
have mercy on me.

As the questions rise in my mind,
have mercy on me.

As the devil tries and tries again,
have mercy on me.

As I fail,
have mercy on me.

As the world groans louder,
have mercy on me.

As worry tries to steal my peace,
have mercy on me.

As afternoon becomes evening,
have mercy on me.

As the sun begins to set,
have mercy on me.

As I exhale and close my eyes to sleep,
have mercy on me.

O God,
have mercy on me.

Lament

O God, I am lost in the wild of my thoughts.
Once again there is sadness in my soul.
I'm searching for light in the darkness, but the darkness
seems to have control.

God, won't You again come close?

Father, take my pain.
Father, take my dismay.
Father, take my suffering.

All of this is too heavy for me to carry.

O God, where are You in this?
Won't You again make Yourself known to the aching and
alone?

Yet, I trust You're creating something
beautiful out of what is broken.

Give my shaking hands the strength to trust You.
Lift my eyes to see where the light comes through.
Place my feet back upon Your firm foundation of hope.

May I only be lost in Your grace.

Thanksgiving

Whatever today brings, may all of this be for the One who holds all things together.
May this be for the One who loves us despite our mess and hears us when we confess.
Slow to anger and quick to patience.
And it's Your patience that I am thankful for.
Despite my sin and shame, You've made a way for us to be with You day after day.
You don't deal with us as we deserve, and in that, I can rest.
I can rest knowing there is hope in all of this.
Hope is what I'll hold on to as You hold on to me.

In the pain and the fear, in the uncertain and unknown, through it all, hope is here.

Teach me to sing Your song slower,
so I can sit longer with Your words,
lose myself in Your melody,
be found in Your faithfulness.

When the morning comes,
I'll remember all You've done.

Wash Over Me

I'm searching for something more than I've found;
planting seeds of hope deep in the ground;
listening for Your voice to make a sound.

Won't You wash over me as I wait?

All I can do is wait.

All I can do is be still and breathe deep
and pray I remember Your grace and peace.

All I can do is look for Your mercy, the same
mercy my eyes find every morning.

In the quiet I am reminded: Your love has always
been chasing after me and going before me.

And it doesn't plan to stop.

I can feel pure light washing over me, like the water
and Word once splashed and spoken over me.

God, is this what it feels like to be free?

Let Today

Turn around to see the steps you took that brought you to be.

Fix your eyes on the grace that led you from place to place.

Trace over the lines and I believe you'll find
courage and mercy led you from what lies behind.

Flip through the photos to see how you've grown
and made it through what was once unknown.

Look back on what has been and remember
He has been and will be with you until the very end.

Let today be a day when looking back leads you forward.

_____

Give thanks to the LORD, for He is good, for His steadfast love endures forever.

PSALM 136:1

More than Before

When I slow down, I see that You
are part of everything.
You invite me to be by Your side
as I make my way through this life.
I'm leaving behind what's keeping me behind.
I'm losing my life to come alive,
and I'm carrying what You've placed in my hands.
I'm following forward,
stumbling and running and learning
the pace of grace.
You remind me
again and again
life is worth living
and with You,
I am living for more.

I'm living for more than before.

An Uncommon Prayer

Heavenly Father,

Thank You for this wound.
Thank You for this setback.
Thank You for this brokenness.
Thank You for this pain.
Thank You for what I did not want
but still needed.
Now, help me.
Help me.

Amen.

May It Be

May it be faith that moves us forward.
May it be peace that passes through our pain.
May it be mercy that meets us in the morning.
May it be love that leads us to take the next step.
May it be joy we leave for others to find.
May it be wisdom that delivers us through the
wild unknown.
May it be hope we hold on to as You continue to
carry us home.

From Morning to Night

Father,

You have brought me into the miracle of another day.

As the world wakes, remove the noise
from my heart and allow me to clearly hear
the sincerity of Your devotion.

Out of Your great compassion,
may I seek justice,
love mercy,
and walk humbly with You from morning to night.

And once again tomorrow.

Amen.

He has told you, O man, what is good; and what does the LORD require of you but to do justice, and to love kindness, and to walk humbly with your God?

MICAH 6:8

Step to Explore

Lift up my eyes from this floor;
give me peace as I step to explore,
knowing where I go You've been before.

My Idea

Slowly I am coming to understand God is bigger than my
idea of who I believe He is.

Just as His love is wider.
Just as His mercy is deeper.
Just as His grace is greater.

May my idea of God align with the truth of God.
May I be confused and awed.
May I be brought to my knees and moved to my feet.
May my mouth be silenced and full of praise.

Open my mind to understand
You are greater than
my idea of who I believe
You are.

A Prayer for a Monday

Lord,

Let it be with hopeful hands
and faithful feet that I begin another week.
As I go may I bring the grace and peace
You've spoken and shared with me to everyone I meet.

Amen.

A Prayer about Generosity

Lord,

Your generosity has not ended.
Through every season and question and celebration,
You've continued to give.
And it's changing me.
Changing how I see You and me and the world You created.
I am learning to receive it all with joy.
All of this is from You.
Even when I don't understand,
it is and always has been from You.
And I don't see Your generosity running out anytime soon.
Like You, it doesn't end.

Amen.

Whole

Take these broken pieces
and make me whole.
The pieces I'm hiding,
the pieces I've lost,
the pieces I've forgotten,
and make me whole.

Therefore, if anyone is in Christ, he is a new creation. The old has passed away; behold, the new has come.

2 CORINTHIANS 5:17

Through It All

Lord,

Most days this side of heaven don't make sense.
Yet, I believe Your goodness still triumphs over my
wondering.
Through all of this may we remember that You are holy.
Through uncertainty and pain.
Through fear and shame.
Through sleepless nights and days that seem to repeat.
Through unanswered questions and feelings of defeat.
Through it all,
You are holy.

Amen.

Silence Be My Prayer

When I cannot find the words,
may silence be my prayer.
I'll sit here and be.
And I have nothing to say today,
but I'll stay.
And I'll sit
right here
before You and
with You.

Because all I really want is to be with You.

To Rest

Lead my soul to rest
in the peace of Your promises.

Open my heart to hope
in the truth of redemption.

Bring my eyes to look up and see
the beauty of becoming.

Every New Day

Every new day I remind myself that this day, the one right in front of me, is a gift.

A beautiful and simple and intricate and loving gift.

A gift thought of long before it ever arrived and I am invited to open it up and come alive.

I am allowed to feel and explore and love and dream and create and cry and try and spread hope and give back and hold on.

I am welcome to rest and write and daydream and forgive and be forgiven and celebrate.

I am invited to walk beneath the sun and sit below the stars and pray out loud or in my head or with my hands.

This day, the one right in front of me, is a gift.

And I will not let it pass away.

Tomorrow Too

Today when I feel afraid,
I will trust You.

Tomorrow too.

Today when I feel alone,
I will remember You are with me.

Tomorrow too.

Today when I feel shame,
I will hold close the promise of grace.

Tomorrow too.

Today when I feel lost,
I will be quick to recall You are the way.

Tomorrow too.

With Love and Grace

Let it be
with heart
with soul
with mind
with strength
that I press on
and move beyond
with love and grace.

Your Patience, O God

Draw me closer than before
for there is a wildfire of fear
chasing after my hope.

Go ahead of me as You have always done.
Step close to my weariness and do as only You do:
bring light to my darkness.

Keep me wrapped in the mystery of grace as I
stumble through this gift of life.

Just like You've been before,
won't You be patient with me?

I know You know I need it.

God, I need You.

I've Been Found

Maybe, just maybe,
as I go through
the continued uncertain
and constant unknown,
I'll learn that what You have for me
is beyond my own plan.

Soon I'll begin to understand
my life is hidden in You
and that means
I am truly found.

And if I am found
I don't need to worry.
Or fear.
Or lose my mind.

I've been found.
From life to death to what's next,
I've been found.

Teach Me

As a new day begins,
may Your steadfast hope give me the faith
to remember Your promises.

Soften what I have come to know;
let it be in Your love I grow.

Open my mouth to confess.
Carry me into a life of less.

Ease my mind and show me the beauty of rest.
In the surrounding silence may I believe
what You have for me is best.

This Isn't the End

In the silence
I will wait with faith
knowing this isn't
the end.

In the dark
I will wait with hope
knowing this isn't
the end.

In the uncertainty
I will wait with love
knowing this isn't
the end.

For where I am,
You are too.

Hallelujah

I never thought this is what all of this would become.
But what it has become isn't bad.
It's different.
But it isn't bad.
It's weird.
But it isn't bad.
It's changing.
It's uncertain.
It's hard.

But it isn't bad.
It isn't bad.
. . . Hallelujah.

It is different.
Hallelujah.
It is weird.
Hallelujah.
It is changing.
It is uncertain.
It is hard.
Hallelujah.

But it isn't bad.
Hallelujah.

Home in My Heart

God,

Make a home in my heart; let me exhale
with peace.
Remove my need for answers,
Replace my desire to be correct.
Let life return to my soul, like when I was a child.
Dismantle and repair and repeat
as only You can do.
Teach me to be me again.
Let me find myself in You.

Amen.

Seasons of Silence

I'll continue to believe
through seasons of silence
that You hear me,
that You see me,
and You are for me.

Everything I Do Matters

I am learning to not give up on myself.
Everything I do matters.
There is purpose in every breath and every step,
every no and every yes.
Your mercy is new every morning,
even this one,
and the one before.
And it will be there tomorrow too.
And tomorrow is a good day to not give up on myself.
Everything I do matters.
This I am coming to believe.

With Faith

Without knowing
what is to come
I'll go with faith
as I continue
to become.

Three in One

Creator, construct in me a heart of wonder.
Christ, fill me with the joy of Your salvation.
Comforter, in the darkness, be the light.

Three in One,
Thy will be done.
May Your kingdom come.

Before You

Before You I have nothing to prove.
Before You I have nothing to fear.
Before You I have nothing to lose.
Before You I have nothing to gain.
You have all I need.

Return to Me

I seem to have,
once again,
misplaced the joy You set inside of me.

Somewhere between the regret
and sorrow
and last Tuesday
it disappeared.

I know it's there,
but this morning
I am struggling to see
and think
and breathe clearly.

God,
I want to see
and think
and breathe clearly.

And I need You.

Return to me the joy of Your resurrection,
the hope of eternity, and the peace
that goes beyond my understanding.

Return to me.

Prayer for Today

May this *amen*
be far from the end.

Throughout the day
may I continue to pray
and thank You for the kindness
of Your unexplainable ways.

Make me more aware of Your goodness
and give me words to praise You for
Your faithfulness.

As I step into the world,
give me the grace to receive
what You have for me
and the wisdom to understand
all things are in Your hands.

By My Side

When the hard and heavy arrives
let faith pump inside,
let love be my guide,
as I trust in and lean on
You by my side.

Finally Free

Rest
and breathe
and believe
you are finally free
because of what
He has done
for you and me.

Forever Reign

Spirit,

Bring me to stand in awe,
to live unashamed for the One who gave His life away.
Draw us out of the darkness,
overcome by Your presence,
and move us beyond imagination,
far from evil and temptation.
Let Your love light every step of the way.
Set a fire in my soul for Your will to be done.
Burn within; forever reign.

Amen.

Whatever

Whatever comes my way,
joy
or pain,
sunshine
or rain,
may I see
and believe
Your love remains
with me.

Make a Way

If I'm chasing wind, bring it all to an end.
Let Your light lead me away; God, just make a way.

I'm far from the man I want to be.
Lost between love and desire,
growing tired from the tearing,
emptied from the taking,
bruised from the breaking,
only praying keeps these hands from shaking.

Again I'm sorry for who I've been,
the boy I was way back when.
I got tripped up by selfishness,
ripped up by restlessness.
I confess my recklessness
and I'm done trying to hide.
I'm done making excuses out of pride.
Won't You again call me back to Your side?

Won't You pull me into the present?
I've been hanging around my past,
but my future needs to be quite the contrast
if I am ever going to make this living last.

I want to make this living last.

I need to hear You say welcome home
and finally believe I am not alone.
Let me rest in grace and wake with faith.

And I know, I know I've said it all before, but with my
knees to the floor, I pray you'll forgive and restore.

God, if I'm chasing wind, bring it all to an end.
Let Your light lead me away; just make a way.

Consider the Wildflowers

And tomorrow when I wake
I'll consider the wildflowers.
Simple and beautiful and cared for.
Seen and celebrated and chosen.
Full of life and color and hope.
Living proof that a seed can become a growing
reminder of change.
Like us.

Consider the lilies, how they grow: they neither toil nor spin, yet I tell you, even Solomon in all his glory was not arrayed like one of these. But if God so clothes the grass, which is alive in the field today, and tomorrow is thrown into the oven, how much more will He clothe you, O you of little faith!

LUKE 12:27–28

Spill Over

May it be wonder.
May it be hope.
May it be promise.
May it be grace.
May it be kindness.
May it be love.
May it be restoration.
May it be peace.
May it be empathy.
May it be mercy.
May it be invitation.
May it be joy.
May it be softness.
May it be faith.

May You keep these things in my heart
and may they spill over into the lives around me.

Deep Within

Deep within I heard You say,
"Come and see."
And so I went.

I left behind this life of mine
only to find
You had something better for me
the entire time.

He said to them, "Come and you will see." So they came and saw where He was staying, and they stayed with Him that day, for it was about the tenth hour. One of the two who heard John speak and followed Jesus was Andrew, Simon Peter's brother. He first found his own brother Simon and said to him, "We have found the Messiah" (which means Christ).

J O H N   1 : 3 9 – 4 1

Through The

Through the pain,
joy remains.

Through the questions,
hope remains.

Through the uncertainty,
mercy remains.

Through the fear,
faith remains.

God, Help Me Remember

Grace is woven through all of this.
From beginning to end and back again.
Through the brokenness and beauty, the questions and answers.
I'm telling myself to remember the hope that has me.
Hope has me.
As heavy as hope is, it has me and keeps me moving forward.
And that's what I need to remember.
Hope has me.
God, help me remember.

Through the Waiting

Through the waiting
and unknown
and wondering when I'll know,
I'll remember this is another season where
You're inviting me to grow.

A Prayer for Wisdom

God,

You alone are worthy of praise.
In You alone we find the courage to wake with the sunrise
and serve till the sunset.
Give me Your wisdom as I move through today.
Go before my words and give grace to my decisions.
Quiet my thoughts to hear Your Spirit speak life and hope
into me.
Guard my mind with peace today and always.

Amen.

Isn't It Something

Isn't it something
that we are called
the one thing
we've always wanted
to be called?

Beloved.

Put on then, as God's chosen ones, holy and beloved, com-
passionate hearts, kindness, humility, meekness, and patience.

COLOSSIANS 3:12

Slow Me Down

Slow me down to breathe
and believe
You will never leave me.
Despite my doubts,
despite the fear that continues to shout,
despite the silence that keeps me from crying out,
You will never leave me.

Holy, Holy, Holy

Put your ear to the sky
and open your hands wide
to hold what heaven
continues to cry:
Holy, holy, holy.

Surrender to the Mystery

I'll never have all the answers.
I'll never have all the correct questions.
Soften my edges; loosen my grip.
Teach these hands
to hold what I can
and to let go of what needs to be put down.
Let me breathe easy and rest
in Your continued kindness,
to finally surrender to the mystery of Your ways
and step into a life of trust.

What Do You Know That I Don't?

I guess this is me just wondering.
And I know, I know if You told us the future
we wouldn't need faith.
If You gave us all the answers it would steal away
the beauty of the mystery.
And God, the mystery is beautiful.

But there is something
in the waiting and the wondering.

There is something for me
in the waiting and the wondering.

But I know You know something I don't.
I know You know everything I don't.

I'm not asking for all the answers, but I'm
wondering, is it going to be okay?

Is it all going to be okay?

Am I going to be okay?

Okay.

Little by Little

Little by little
You are showing me
You are part
of every little thing.

I am learning
to praise You
in seasons
I wish would pass.

I am beginning
to thank You
for the things
I do not want.

I have started stumbling
upon joy in the darkness,
hope in the confusion,
and love in the face of fear.

If You are part
of every little thing,
certainly You are with me
in this.

And You will certainly be with me
in whatever comes next.

Guided by Gentleness

Guide me with gentleness.
Quietly calm my fears
and call me from chaos
with faith.
In storms and waves,
remind me, like Peter,
"Do not be afraid."
May I be still in Your silence.
May I be moved by Your mercy.
And like You've done again and again,
keep me from sinking.

Them Too

Open my eyes to see
You call them Beloved too.

Open my heart to believe
You extend grace to them too.

Open my hands to receive
the forgiveness You freely give to them too.

Open my ears to hear You love them too.

And so should I.

I'm Still Here Alive

I'm still here alive
and I know
despite the fear the world cries
I will never die.

My last breath
will be my first gasp of eternal life.
Washed white by the blood of the Lamb.
Raised to stand in the presence of the holy I AM.

As I wait to be welcomed to heaven's side,
hope keeps me alive.
A fire growing inside.
A love burning bright.
My past erased by His light.
My future is hidden in Christ.

I'll forever be resurrected and alive
with the taste of eternity on my lips.

This new life wrapped in grace upon grace,
singing holy in the presence of His continued glory.
I believe what I cannot understand:
my soul forever found in His hands.
I'm still here alive.

Your Kindness Is Unlike Any Other

Let me live in the echo of Your unending love,
walking in the promise of eternity,
knowing that You have always had something more
for me and my wondering.

May the rhythms of grace bring joy to my unknown
and in my questioning
may I remember
You've called me Yours.

Though I've caused pain and done wrong,
You did not turn from me but
toward me.

Again and again You speak love over me
with kindness unlike any other.

Distant and Disconnected

When I feel distant and
disconnected
may Your grace guide me to remember
I am not a burden and
Your mercies will be new again in the morning.

I Believe

Tomorrow when the sun comes up
I'll exhale and pray
I believe
help my unbelief.
The same five words
I prayed
this morning.
Every day I pray
I believe
help my unbelief.

Soften My Heart

Soften my heart
and let me believe
that even though there is silence
You are still with me.

Soften my heart
and open my ears
to hear You
meeting my fear.

Soften my heart
and bring me to see
faith does not require clarity.

Translate

Here, with You, I am reaching for help.
Scattered thanks and muddled reflections.
My confession is all over the place,
full of pauses
and promises
and I ask once again for You to forgive me.
And You do.

I give You my stillness and silence and screams.
My words are for You, but they do not earn You.
You are already with me and for me and ahead of me.
My silence is received the same as my thanks
and today all I have is something somewhere in between.
You translate the quiet I hold and clearly understand my
broken sentences that don't seem to start or end.
You know me.

Through it all, grace finds a way.
You continue to love me the same,
my help and my salvation.

Benediction

Holy Father,

As we continue,
may Your strength sustain us,
may Your power preserve us,
may Your grace guide us,
and may Your love go with us now and forever.

Amen.

End of the Day

Holy God,

Slow me down to speak what I've come to pray.
Hear my prayer, the words I cannot seem to find and the
ones I lay before You.

I thank You for the gift of another day
and the courage You placed in me
that led me forward and through.
I praise You for Your protection and love.
As hard as this sometimes is to say, I am grateful
for what was, what is, and what is becoming.

As today becomes tomorrow, may I know You
and may I know myself in You and in You alone.
Give me eyes to see me how You see me.
Move my feet in the confident hope of eternity.
Make my heart like Yours, full of love and compassion and
invitation.

To You, I surrender all I have.

Fill me with Your Spirit.
Send me with Your Word.
Guide me with Your grace.

Amen.

EPILOGUE

Anyway

There always seems to be more than one thing
happening at once.
I write of hope and love and peace, but
throughout the day those words can feel
far and foreign to me.

I'm learning that I can feel and believe more than
one thing at a time.

When I am sad, I will be sad.
When I am angry, I will be angry.
When I am confused, I will be confused.
When I am scared, I will be scared.

Yet . . .
When I am sad, I'll cling to hope.
When I am angry, I'll remember I am loved and invited to
live out love.
When I am confused, I'll praise God.
When I am scared, I'll continue.

No matter what,
I'll hope anyway.
I'll love anyway.
I'll praise anyway.
I'll continue anyway.